I0648041

Given to me
by Valerie Bloemeke
may, 2005

To:

_____

From:

_____

The fruit of the Spirit is love,
joy, peace, patience, kindness,
goodness, faithfulness,
gentleness, and self-control.

GALATIANS 5:22–23

Family Christian Press is a division of Family Christian Stores,
5300 Patterson Ave SE, Grand Rapids, MI 49530

Family Christian Press is a trademark of Family Christian Stores

Project management and compilation: Molly C. Detweiler
Design: Mark Veldheer
Photography: Brad Lampe/Synergy Photographic

Printed in the United States of America

Abundance
of the Spirit

for
women

FCP

FAMILY
CHRISTIAN
PRESS

Table *of* Contents

love

*L*ove is patient, love is kind. It does not envy, it does not boast, it is not proud. It is not rude, it is not self-seeking, it is not easily angered, it keeps no record of wrongs. Love does not delight in evil but rejoices with the truth. It always protects, always trusts, always hopes, always perseveres. Love never fails.

1 CORINTHIANS 13:4–8

WHAT DOES "I LOVE YOU" LOOK LIKE?

I was blessed. I began to learn to see God from the moment I was born. God is love, and the first thing I knew was what "I love you" looked like.

As a small child, I saw God in my mother. She was always there with open arms to hold me. She never failed to feed me when I was hungry, to warm me when I was cold, and to care for me when I was sick. She didn't just say, "I love you"—she showed me what "I love you" looks like.

I also saw God in my father. He worked hard every day to make sure I was well cared for. He protected me in his strong arms. He laughed with me over cartoons and silly jokes. He took me to the park and for walks in the woods so I could see the beauty of God's world for myself. He didn't just say, "I love you"—he showed me what "I love you" looks like.

As I grew up, God showed up in the love of many other people. My grandparents showed me God through their prayers, their thoughtful gifts, and through the stories of their encounters with God's love.

God gave me friends to show me his love. They played with me, listened to my secrets, and shared their secrets with me. They helped me with homework and allowed me to help them in turn.

I saw God in my teachers sometimes, too. Every day they guided me in learning so many things and encouraged me with kind words and gentle discipline.

All these people, in so many ways, showed me what "I love you" looks like.

One beautiful spring, God's love came to me in a new and wonderful way. I met a young man who spent hours talking with me and listening to my hopes and dreams. He rejoiced with me in my joys and was there with comfort when I cried.

One beautiful spring, a few years later, that man promised to be with me forever and to always love me only. My husband didn't just say "I love you"—he showed me what it looks like.

And now, I'm all grown up. I've been blessed with glimpses of the God of love in so many ways. But as I look around I see that those glimpses are harder to find in the world around me. I see that many people do not know what "I love you" looks like. Many people don't even hear the words.

But a long time ago, Jesus gave up everything, including his own life, to show us all what "I love you" looks like. So now, my hope and prayer is that my life will do the same.

Molly Detweiler

Love is the doorway through which the human soul passes from selfishness to service and from solitude to kinship with all mankind.

Who can separate us from Christ's love? Can trouble or hard times or harm or hunger? Can nakedness or danger or war?...

No! In all these things we will do even more than win! We owe it all to Christ, who has loved us. I am absolutely sure that not even death or life can separate us from God's love. Not even angels or demons, the present or the future, or any powers can do that. Not even the highest places or the lowest, or anything else in all creation can do that. Nothing at all can ever separate us from God's love because of what Christ Jesus our Lord has done.

Romans 8:35, 37–39 NIrV

*Love is
the beauty
of
the soul.*

AUGUSTINE OF HIPPO

And now these three remain: faith, hope and love. But the greatest of these is love.

1 Corinthians 13:13

Whoever loves true life, will love true love.

Elizabeth Barrett Browning

God chose us in him before the creation of the world to be holy and blameless in his sight. In love he predestined us to be adopted as his sons through Jesus Christ, in accordance with his pleasure and will—to the praise of his glorious grace, which he has freely given us in the One he loves.

Ephesians 1:4–6

I was taught that love is our Lord's meaning, and I saw most certainly in this and in all things that before God made us He loved us; this love was never diminished nor shall it ever be. And in His love He has accomplished all His works; and in this love He has made all things profitable to us; and in this love our life is everlasting.

In our creation, we had a beginning, but the love out of which He made us was always within Him. In this love we have our beginning and in all this we shall see God eternally.

Lady Julian of Norwich

Accustom yourself continually to make many acts of love, for they enkindle and melt the soul.

Teresa of Avila

GOD IS IN LOVE WITH US

Eternal Father, you said, "Let us make humankind to our own image and likeness." Thus you were willing to share with us your own greatness. You gave us the intellect to share your truth. You gave us the wisdom to share your goodness. And you gave us the free will to love that which is true and just.

Why did you so dignify us? It was because you looked upon us, and fell in love with us. It was love which first prompted you to create us; and it was love which caused you to share with us your truth and goodness.

Yet your heart must break when you see us turn against you. You must weep when you see us abusing our intellect in pursuit of that which is false. You must cry with pain when we distort our wisdom in order to justify evil.

But you never desert us. Out of the same love that caused you to create us, you have now sent your only Son to save us. He is your perfect image and likeness, and so through him we can be restored to your image and likeness.

Catherine of Siena

People are renewed by love.
As sinful desire ages them,
so love rejuvenates them.

Augustine of Hippo

Praise the LORD, O my soul,
*   and forget not all his benefits —*
who forgives all your sins
*   and heals all your diseases,*
who redeems your life from the pit
*   and crowns you with love and compassion,*
who satisfies your desires with good things
*   so that your youth is renewed like the eagle's.*

Psalm 103:2–5

God so loved the world that he gave his one and only Son, that whoever believes in him shall not perish but have eternal life.

John 3:16

Love feels no burden, thinks nothing of trouble, attempts what is above its strength, pleads no excuse of impossibility; for it thinks all things lawful for itself, and all things possible.

Thomas à Kempis

Jesus said, "'Love the Lord your God with all your heart and with all your soul and with all your mind.' This is the first and greatest commandment. And the second is like it: 'Love your neighbor as yourself.'"

Matthew 22:37–39

*To love
another person
is to see the
face of God.*

VICTOR HUGO

Some of us know what it is to love, and we know that could we only have our way, our beloved ones would be overwhelmed with blessings. All that is good, and sweet, and lovely in life would be poured out upon them from our lavish hands, had we but the power to carry out our will for them. And if this is the way of love with us, how much more must it be so with our God, who is love itself.

Hannah Whitall Smith

O Love that will not let me go,
I rest my weary soul in thee,
I give thee back the life I owe,
That in thine ocean depths its flow
May richer, fuller, be.

George Matheson

The LORD appeared to us in the past, saying:
"I have loved you with an everlasting love;
I have drawn you with loving-kindness."

Jeremiah 31:3

Nothing binds me to my Lord like a strong belief in his changeless love.

C.H. Spurgeon

I pray that out of his glorious riches he may strengthen you with power through his Spirit in your inner being, so that Christ may dwell in your hearts through faith. And I pray that you, being rooted and established in love, may have power, together with all the saints, to grasp how wide and long and high and deep is the love of Christ, and to know this love that surpasses knowledge — that you may be filled to the measure of all the fullness of God.

Ephesians 3:16–19

joy

*t*he LORD has done

great things for us,

and we are filled with joy.

PSALM 126:3

MAY 13, 1657

As spring the winter does succeed
    And leaves the naked trees do dress,
The earth all black is clothed in green.
    At sunshine each their joy express.

My sun's returned with healing wings,
    My soul and body doth rejoice,
My heart exults and praises sings
    To him that heard my wailing voice.

My winter's past, my storms are gone,
    And former clouds seem not all fled,
But if they must eclipse again,
    I'll run where I was succored.

I have a shelter from the storm,
    A shadow from the fainting heat,
I have access unto his throne,
    Who is a God so wondrous great.

O have thou made my pilgrimage
    Thus pleasant, fair, and good,
Blessed in youth and elder age,
    My Baca made a springing flood.

O studious I am what I shall do
    To show my duty with delight;
All I can give is but thine own
    And at the most a simple mite.

Anne Bradstreet

Flow on, Thou Fountain of my joy
  Through all the wilderness!
Thou seest what will work for good,
  Thou knowest how to bless.

Anna L. Waring

*You have made known to me the path of life;
  you will fill me with joy in your
      presence, LORD,
  with eternal pleasures at your right hand.*

Psalm 16:11

The fullness of joy is in God's immediate presence.

Richard Baxter

*Joy is the
echo of
God's life
within us.*

JOSEPH MARMION

Christ is not only a remedy for your weariness and trouble, but he will give you an abundance of the contrary, joy and delight.

Jonathan Edwards

The Spirit of the Sovereign LORD...
    has sent me to bind up the brokenhearted,...
to comfort all who mourn,
    and provide for those who grieve in Zion —
to bestow on them a crown of beauty
    instead of ashes,
the oil of gladness
    instead of mourning.

Isaiah 61:1–3

There is not one blade of grass, there is no color in this world that is not intended to make us rejoice.

John Calvin

When Jesus is present, all is well, and nothing seems difficult.

Thomas à Kempis

27

ALL THINGS SHALL BE WELL

One time our Lord said to me, "All things shall be well." And another time he said, "You yourself shall see that all manner of things shall be well," and my soul understood these two sayings to mean several different things.

One meaning was that his will is for us to know that he takes notice not only of great and noble things, but of little and small things as well, low and simple things, one and the other. And so this is what he meant by saying, "All manner of things shall be well." For it is his will that we know even the smallest of things will not be forgotten.

Another meaning was this: We see many evil deeds done all around us, deeds that cause great harm, and sometimes it seems impossible that they should ever result in anything good. Sometimes we see these evils, sorrowing and mourning

because of them, we find it difficult to
concentrate on beholding God blissfully,
which is something we should do. And the
cause of this is that our reasoning capacity
is now so blind, low, and simple that we
cannot know his high and marvelous
wisdom, the power and the goodness of
the blissful Trinity. And this is what he
meant when he said, "You yourself shall
see that all manner of things shall be well."
It was as if he had said, "Take heed faith-
fully and trustingly now, and at the end of
all things, you will truly see them in the
fullness of joy."

Lady Julian of Norwich

One inch of joy
surmounts grief a span.

Francis Rabelais

The LORD is my strength and my shield;
  my heart trusts in him, and I am helped.
My heart leaps for joy
  and I will give thanks to him in song.

Psalm 28:7

You are the fullness and unfailing
plenty of unfading joys.... You are
the most lavish giver of all good.

St. Augustine

God's gifts

put man's

best dreams

to shame.

ELIZABETH BARRETT BROWNING

Jesus said, "I tell you the truth, you will weep and mourn while the world rejoices. You will grieve, but your grief will turn to joy.... Now is your time of grief, but I will see you again and you will rejoice, and no one will take away your joy."

John 16:20, 22

If a person has sought first and chiefly the soul's treasure—goodness, kindness, gentleness, devoutness, cheerfulness, hope, faith, and love— he will extract more joy from the poorest furniture and outfitting of life than otherwise he would get from the whole world.

Henry Ward Beecher

Weeping may remain for a night,
but rejoicing comes in the morning.

Psalm 30:5

Today, whatever may annoy,
The word for me is Joy, just simple Joy.
Whate'er there be of Sorrow
I'll put off till Tomorrow,
And when Tomorrow comes, why then
'Twill be Today and Joy again.

John Kendrick Bangs

peace

Jesus said, "Peace I leave with you; my peace I give you. I do not give to you as the world gives. Do not let your hearts be troubled and do not be afraid."

JOHN 14:27

THE BEAUTY OF REST

Among the peaks of the Sierra Nevada mountains, not far from the busy whirl of San Francisco, lies Lake Tahoe. It is twenty-three miles long, ten miles wide, and so deep that a line dropped nineteen hundred feet does not touch the bottom; and it lies five thousand feet above the neighboring ocean. Storms come and go in waters that are lower down the mountains, but this lake is so still and clear that the eye can penetrate, it is said, a hundred feet into its depths. Around its mild verdant sides are the mountains, ever crowned with snow. The sky above is as calm as the motionless water. Nature loses scarcely anything of its clear outline as it is reflected there. Here the soul may learn something of what rest is, as day after day one opens one's heart to let the sweet influence of nature's Sabbath enter and reign.

This is but a faint type of what we may find in Christ.

In the pressure of the greatest responsibilities, in the worry of the smallest cares, in the perplexities of life's moments of crisis, we may have the Lake Tahoe rest in the security of God's will. Learn to live in this rest. In the calmness of spirit it will give, your soul will reflect, as in a mirror, the beauty of the Lord; and the tumult of men's lives will be calmed in your presence, as your tumults have been calmed in his presence.

Hannah Whitall Smith

Drop thy still dews of quietness till all our
    striving cease;
Take from our souls the strain and stress,
And let our ordered lives confess
The beauty of thy Peace.

John Greenleaf Whittier

I smiled to think God's greatness
flowed around our incompleteness.
Round our restlessness His rest.

Elizabeth Barrett Browning

*The LORD bless you
    and keep you;
the LORD make his face shine upon you
    and be gracious to you;
the LORD turn his face toward you
    and give you peace.*

Numbers 6:24–26

Peace reigns where our Lord reigns.

LADY JULIAN OF NORWICH

Like a river glorious is God's perfect peace,
Over all victorious in its bright increase;
Perfect, yet it floweth fuller every day,
Perfect, yet it groweth deeper all the way.
Stayed upon Jehovah, hearts are fully blest;
Finding, as he promised, perfect peace
    and rest.

Frances Ridley Havergal

*Jesus said, "In this world you
will have trouble. But take heart!
I have overcome the world."*

John 16:33

When Christ came into the world, peace
was sung; and when he went out of the
world, peace was bequested.

Francis Bacon

If God be our God, He will give us peace in trouble. When there is a storm without, He will make peace within. The world can create trouble in peace, but God can create peace in trouble.

Thomas Watson

You will keep in perfect peace him whose mind is steadfast, because he trusts in you, O LORD.

Isaiah 26:3

THE PEACE OF TRUST

The beloved hymn, *'Tis So Sweet to Trust in Jesus*, was written by Louisa M.R. Stead.

As a young woman, growing up in England, Louisa felt passionately that God was calling her to the mission field. When she was only 21 she traveled across the ocean to the United States and lived in Ohio for a time. During a camp meeting one evening she heard God's call to ministry again. She felt more strongly than ever that she was meant to take the gospel to a far-off land. In particular, she longed to sail to China to share the Good News of Jesus.

Sadly, though, Louisa was not in good health and in spite of her strong desire to be a missionary, she found herself unable to travel abroad. Her disappointment was turned to joy, however, when in 1875 she was married, and when, soon after, she became the mother of a daughter she named Lily.

Young Louisa had been married just five years when tragedy struck and she once again faced the destruction of her hopes and dreams. Louisa's husband lost his life saving their four-year-old Lily from drowning. As she mourned, asking God why this had happened, she was blessed with his whispers of peace. The beautiful words of *'Tis So Sweet to Trust in Jesus* came to her in the midst of her grief.

And in 1880, Louisa experienced the fruit of her trust in the Lord when she traveled to South Africa to serve as a missionary, fulfilling the call she had received as a young girl. She served in Africa for 15 years, was remarried, and saw her daughter Lily become a missionary, like her mother.

'Tis so sweet to trust in Jesus,
Just to take Him at His word,
Just to rest upon His promise,
Just to know, "Thus saith the Lord."

I'm so glad I learned to trust Thee,
Precious Jesus, Savior, Friend;
And I know that Thou art with me,
Wilt be with me to the end.

Jesus, Jesus, how I trust Him!
How I've proved Him o'er and o'er!
Jesus, Jesus, precious Jesus!
O for grace to trust Him more!

*I will lie down and sleep in peace,
for you alone, O LORD,
make me dwell in safety.*

Psalm 4:8

You touched me, Lord, and I am
inflamed with love of your peace.

St. Augustine

*May the God of hope fill you
with all joy and peace as you
trust in him, so that you may
overflow with hope by the power
of the Holy Spirit.*

Romans 15:13

The mind controlled by the Spirit is life and peace.

ROMANS 8:6

Peace does not dwell in outward things, but within the soul.

François Fénelon

The LORD gives strength to his people; the LORD blesses his people with peace.

Psalm 29:11

Let nothing disturb thee,
Nothing frighten thee;
All things are passing;
God never changes.
Patient endurance
Attains all things;
Who God possesses
In nothing is wanting;
Alone God suffices.

Teresa of Avila

Do not be anxious about anything, but in everything, by prayer and petition, with thanksgiving, present your requests to God. And the peace of God, which transcends all understanding, will guard your hearts and your minds in Christ Jesus.

Philippians 4:6–7

O God, make us children of quietness, and heirs of peace.

Clement of Rome

patience

We pray...that you may live a life worthy of the Lord and may please him in every way: bearing fruit in every good work, growing in the knowledge of God, being strengthened with all power according to his glorious might so that you may have great endurance and patience.

Colossians 1:10–11

The Hand of God
Also Waits

Did you ever hear of anyone being much used for Christ who did not have some special waiting time, some complete upset of all his or her plans first; from St. Paul's being sent off into the desert of Arabia for three years, when he must have been boiling over with the glad tidings, down to the present day?

You were looking forward to telling about trusting Jesus in Syria; now he says, "I want you to show what it is to trust me, without waiting for Syria."

My own case is far less severe, but the same principle, that when I thought the door was flung open for me to go with a bound into literary work, it is opposed, and the doctor steps in and says, simply, "Never! She must choose between writing and living; she can't do both!"

In 1869 I saw the evident wisdom of being kept waiting nine years in the shade. God's love being unchangeable, he is just as loving when we do not see or feel his love. Also his love and his sovereignty are co-equal and universal; so he withholds the enjoyment and conscious progress because he knows best what will really ripen and further his work in us.

Frances Ridley Havergal

I waited patiently for the LORD;
he turned to me and heard my cry.
He lifted me out of the slimy pit,
out of the mud and mire;
he set my feet on a rock
and gave me a firm place to stand.
He put a new song in my mouth,
a hymn of praise to our God.
Many will see and fear
and put their trust in the LORD.

Psalm 40:1–3

The great believers have been the unwearied waiters.

Author Unknown

Anyone who is patient has great understanding.

PROVERBS 14:29 NIrV

Patience and perseverance have a magical effect before which difficulties disappear and obstacles vanish.

John Quincy Adams

Obedience is the fruit of faith; patience the bloom on the fruit.

Christina Rosetti

Hope that is seen is no hope at all. Who hopes for what he already has? But if we hope for what we do not yet have, we wait for it patiently.

Romans 8:24–25

Patience and diligence, like faith, remove mountains.

William Penn

Rest in the Lord; wait patiently for Him. In Hebrew, "Be silent in God, and let Him mold thee." Keep still, and He will mold thee to the right shape.

Martin Luther

True patience grows with the growth of love.

Gregory the Great

PATIENCE AND HOPE

It is the wholesome precept of our Lord and Master: "He that endures," he says, "unto the end shall be saved"; and again, "If you continue," he says, "in my word you will be truly my disciples; and you shall know the truth, and the truth shall make you free." We must endure and persevere, beloved, in order that, being admitted to the hope of truth and liberty, we may attain to the truth and liberty itself; for that very fact that we are Christians is the substance of faith and hope. But if hope and faith are to attain to their result, there is need of patience.

For we are not following after present glory, but future, according to what Paul the apostle says, "We are saved by hope; but hope that is seen is not hope: for what a man sees, why does he hope for?

But if we hope for that which we see not, then we do by patience wait for it." Therefore, waiting and patience are needful, that we may fulfill that which we have begun to be, and may receive that which we believe and hope for. So that he who strives toward the crown with the praise now near at hand, may be crowned by the continuance of patience.

Cyprian

Endurance is the crowning quality,
And patience all the passion of
    great hearts.

James Russell Lowell

*Be patient . . . until the Lord's coming. See how
the farmer waits for the land to yield its valuable
crop and how patient he is for the autumn and
spring rains. You too, be patient and stand firm,
because the Lord's coming is near.*

James 5:7–8

The greatest prayer
is patience.

Author Unknown

Good things come to those who wait.

ANCIENT PROVERB

Patience is not passive; on the contrary, it is active; it is concentrated strength.

Anonymous

Let patience have her perfect work. Statue under the chisel of the sculptor, stand steady to the blows of his mallet. Clay on the wheel, let the fingers of the divine potter model you at their will. Obey the Father's lightest word; hear the Brother who knows you, and died for you.

George Macdonald

Faith takes up the cross, love binds it to the soul, patience bears it to the end.

Horatius Bonar

In the morning, O LORD, you hear my voice;
in the morning I lay my requests before you
and wait in expectation.

Psalm 5:3

I wait for you, O LORD;
you will answer, O LORD
my God.

Psalm 38:15

The LORD longs to be gracious to you;
he rises to show you compassion.
For the LORD is a God of justice.
Blessed are all who wait for him!

Isaiah 30:18

kindness

*b*e kind and compassionate to one another, forgiving each other, just as in Christ God forgave you. Be imitators of God, therefore, as dearly loved children and live a life of love, just as Christ loved us and gave himself up for us as a fragrant offering and sacrifice to God.

EPHESIANS 4:32–5:2

Beautiful Feet

Our Lord has many uses for what is kept for himself. How beautiful are the feet of them that bring glad tidings of good things! That is the best use of all, and I expect the angels think those feet beautiful, even if they are cased in muddy boots or galoshes.

If we want to have these beautiful feet, we must have the tidings ready which they are to bear. Let us ask him to keep our hearts so freshly full of his good news of salvation that our mouths may speak out of their abundance. If the clouds be full of rain, they empty themselves upon the earth. May we be so filled with the Spirit that we may have much to pour out for others.

Besides the privilege of carrying water from the wells of salvation, there are plenty of cups of cold water to be carried in all directions; not to the poor only—ministries of love are often as much needed by a rich friend. But the feet must be kept for these; they will be too tired for them if they are tired out for self-pleasing. In such services we are treading in the blessed steps of Christ, who went about doing good.

Frances Ridley Havergal

A kind heart is a fountain of gladness, making everything in its vicinity freshen into smiles.

Washington Irving

The right kind of heart is a kind heart like God's.

Author Unknown

An anxious heart weighs a man down, a kind word cheers him up.

Proverbs 12:25

No act of kindness, no matter how small, is ever wasted.

Aesop

A

kindhearted

woman gains

respect.

PROVERBS 11:16

Anyone who gives a lot will succeed.
  Anyone who renews others will be renewed.

Proverbs 11:25 NIrV

The person who sows seeds of kindness enjoys a perpetual harvest.

Author Unknown

Give, and it will be given to you. A good measure, pressed down, shaken together and running over, will be poured into your lap. For with the measure you use, it will be measured to you.

Luke 6:38

'Twas a thief that said the last
     kind word to Christ:
Christ took the kindness and
     forgave the theft.

Robert Browning

Kind words are the music of the world. They
have a power which seems to be beyond
natural causes, as if they were some angel's
song which had lost its way and come on
earth. It seems as if they could almost do
what in reality God alone can do — soften the
hard and angry hearts of men.

Frederick William Faber

The heart benevolent and kind
The most resembles God.

Robert Burns

Lord, Speak to Me, That I May Speak

Lord, speak to me, that I may speak
   In living echoes of thy tone;
As thou hast sought, so let me seek
   Thy erring children lost and lone.

O teach me, Lord, that I may teach
   The precious things thou dost
      impart;
And wing my words, that they
      may reach
   The hidden depths of many a heart.

O fill me with thy fullness, Lord,
   Until my very heart o'erflow
In kindling thought and glowing
      word,
   Thy love to tell, thy praise to show.

O use me, Lord, use even me,
   Just as thou wilt, and when
      and where;
Until thy blessed face I see,
   Thy rest, thy joy, thy glory share.

Frances Ridley Havergal

On that best portion of a good
   man's life,
His little, nameless,
   unremembered acts
Of kindness and of love.

William Wordsworth

*"With everlasting kindness
   I will have compassion on you,"
says the LORD your Redeemer.*

Isaiah 54:8

Life is short, and we have never too
much time for gladdening the hearts
of those who are traveling the dark
journey with us. Oh, be swift to love,
make haste to be kind!

Henri Frédérick Amiel

A kind word

is like a

spring day.

RUSSIAN PROVERB

Blessed is the person who is kind to those in need.

Proverbs 14:21 NIrV

The ministry of kindness is a ministry which may be achieved by all, rich and poor, learned and illiterate. Brilliance of mind and capacity for deep thinking have rendered great service to humanity, but by themselves they are powerless to dry a tear or mend a broken heart.

Anonymous

Anyone who is kind to poor people lends to the LORD.
God will reward him for what he has done.

Proverbs 19:17 NIrV

When the kindness and love of God our Savior appeared, he saved us, not because of righteous things we had done, but because of his mercy. He saved us through the washing of rebirth and renewal by the Holy Spirit, whom he poured out on us generously through Jesus Christ our Savior, so that, having been justified by his grace, we might become heirs having the hope of eternal life.

Titus 3:4–7

The greatest thing anyone can do for his heavenly Father is to be kind to some of his other children.

Henry Drummond

goodness

*G*od's divine power has

given us everything we need

for life and godliness

through our knowledge of

him who called us by his

own glory and goodness.

2 PETER 1:3

TRUST IN THE GOODNESS OF GOD

The best and highest use of your mind is to learn to distrust yourself, to renounce your own will, to submit to the will of God, and to become as a little child. It is not of doing difficult things that I speak, but of performing the most common actions with your heart fixed on God. You will be moderate in [your eating habits], moderate in speaking, moderate in [spending], moderate in judging [others], moderate in your [leisure time]; sober even in your wisdom and foresight. It is this universal sobriety in the use of the best things that is taught us by the true love of God. We are neither austere, nor fretful, nor [overly] scrupulous, but have within ourselves a principle of love that enlarges the heart and sheds a gentle influence upon everything; that without constraint or effort, inspires a delicate apprehension lest we should displease God; and that [stops] us if we are tempted to do wrong.

We suffer, as other people do, from fatigue, embarrassments, misfortunes, bodily infirmities, trials from ourselves and trials from others, temptations, disgusts, and sometimes discouragements. But though our crosses are the same with those of the rest of the world, our motives for [enduring] them are very different. We have learned from Jesus Christ how to endure. This can purify, this can detach us from self and renew the spirit of our minds. We see God in everything, but we have the clearest vision of him in suffering and in our humiliations.

Put your trust not in your resolutions or your own strength, but in the goodness of God, who has loved you when you thought not of him, and before you could love him.

François Fénelon

Good nature is one of the richest fruits of Christianity.

Henry Ward Beecher

Surely goodness and love will follow me
all the days of my life,
and I will dwell in the house of the LORD
forever.

Psalm 23:6

In his love God clothes us, enfolds and embraces us; that tender love completely surrounds us, never to leave us. As I see it he is everything that is good.

Lady Julian of Norwich

*Make every
effort to add
to your
faith goodness.*

2 PETER 1:5

Anyone who does what is good is from God.

3 John 1:11

By desiring what is perfectly good, even when we don't quite know what it is and cannot do what we would, we are part of the divine power against evil—widening the skirts of light and making the struggle with darkness narrower.

George Eliot

[Some people], like seed sown on good soil, hear the word, accept it, and produce a crop—thirty, sixty or even a hundred times what was sown.

Mark 4:20

Good, the more
Communicated, more abundant
   grows.

John Milton

Virtue is bold, and goodness
is never fearful.

William Shakespeare

Your actions in passing, pass not
away, for every good work is a
grain of seed for eternal life.

St. Bernard of Clairvaux

THERE IS NO LAW FOR THOSE WHO ARE GOOD

Sons are not outside the law. But you must know that the law given in a spirit of slavery by fear is different from the law of freedom given in gentleness. Children are not under fear, but they cannot survive without love.

Do you wish to hear why there is no law for those who are good? Scripture says, "You did not receive a spirit that makes you a slave again to fear, but you received the Spirit of sonship" (Romans 8:15). The just man says of himself that he is not under the law and yet not free of the law. He says, "To those under the law I became like one under the law (though I myself am not under the law), so as to win those under the law. To those not having the law I became like one not having the law (though I am not free from God's law but am under Christ's law), so as to win those not having the law" (1 Corinthians 9:20–21).

So it is not right to say, "The just have no law," or, "The just are outside the law," but "The law is not made for the just," that is, it is not imposed on them against their will, but freely given to them when they are willing, and inspired by goodness. So the Lord says beautifully, "Take my yoke upon you" (Matthew 11:29), as if he said, "I do not impose it on the unwilling; but you take it if you want to; otherwise you will find not rest but labor for your souls."

St. Bernard of Clairvaux

There's a further good conceivable
Beyond the utmost earth can realize.

Robert Browning

*If you suffer for doing good and
you endure it, this is commendable
before God.*

1 Peter 2:20

Did it ever strike you that goodness is not
merely a beautiful thing, but by far the most
beautiful thing in the whole world? So that
nothing is to be compared for value with
goodness; that riches, honor, power, pleasure,
learning, the whole world and all in it, are
not worth having in comparison with being
good; and the utterly best thing for a man or
woman is to be good, even though they were
never rewarded for it.

Charles Kingsley

*The heart of
the good is
the sanctuary
of God.*

ANNE GERMAINE DE STAEL

Let your light shine before men, that they may see your good deeds and praise your Father in heaven.

Matthew 5:16

Goodness is love in action, love with its hand to the plow, love with the burden on its back, love following his footsteps who went about continually doing good.

James Hamilton

The good man brings good things out of the good stored up in him.

Matthew 12:35

Do all the good you can,
By all the means you can,
In all the ways you can,
In all the places you can,
At all the times you can,
To all the people you can,
As long as ever you can.

John Wesley

To those who by persistence in doing good seek glory, honor and immortality, God will give eternal life.

Romans 2:7

faithfulness

*L*et love and faithfulness

never leave you;

bind them around your neck,

write them on the tablet of

your heart.

PROVERBS 3:3

TRAINING IN FAITHFULNESS

God is ever seeking to teach us the way of faith, and in our training in the faith life there must be room for the trial of faith, the discipline of faith, the patience of faith, and often many stages are passed before we really realize what is the end of faith, namely, the victory of faith.

Real moral fiber is developed through discipline of faith. You have made your request of God, but the answer does not come. What are you to do?

Keep on believing God's Word; never be moved away from it by what you see or feel, and thus as you stand steady, enlarged power and experience is being developed. The fact of looking at the apparent contradiction to God's Word and yet being unmoved from your position of faith make you stronger on every other line.

Often God delays purposely, and the delay is just as much an answer to your prayer as is the fulfillment when it comes.

In the lives of all the great Bible characters, God worked thus. Abraham, Moses, and Elijah were not great in the beginning, but were made great through the discipline of their faith, and only thus were they fitted for the positions to which God had called them.

For example, in the case of Joseph whom the Lord was training for the throne of Egypt, it was not the prison life with its hard beds or poor food that tried him, but it was the word God had spoken into his heart in the early years concerning elevation and honor which were greater than his brethren were to receive; it was this which was ever before him, when every step in his career made it seem more and more impossible of fulfillment. These were hours that tried his soul, but hours of spiritual growth and development.

No amount of persecution tries like such experiences as these. When God has spoken of his purpose to do, and yet the days go on and he does not do it, that is truly hard; but it is a discipline of faith that will bring us into a knowledge of God which would otherwise be impossible.

Mrs. Charles E. Cowman

O Lord my God,
Give me understanding to know you,
Diligence to seek you,
Wisdom to find you,
And a faithfulness that may finally
    embrace you.

Thomas Aquinas

*The LORD rewards everyone for doing
what is right and being faithful.*

1 Samuel 26:23 NIrV

Faith is the wire that connects
you to grace, and over which
grace comes streaming from God.

Anonymous

The faithful
person lives
constantly
with God.

CLEMENT OF ALEXANDRIA

Faith is to believe, on the word
of God, what we do not see, and
its reward is to see and enjoy
what we believe.

St. Augustine

Faithfulness springs forth from the earth,
and righteousness looks down from heaven.

Psalm 85:11

Faith, mighty faith, the
   promise sees
And rests on that alone:
Laughs at impossibilities,
And says it shall be done.

Charles Wesley

If the blind put their hand in God's, they find their way more surely than those who see but have not faith nor purpose.

Helen Keller

Jesus said, "Be faithful, even to the point of death, and I will give you the crown of life."

Revelation 2:10

Faith is a living, bold trust in God's grace, so certain of God's favor that it would risk death a thousand times trusting in it.

Martin Luther

A Good and Faithful Servant

Jesus told this parable: "A man going on a journey... called his servants and entrusted his property to them. To one he gave five talents of money, to another two talents, and to another one talent, each according to his ability. Then he went on his journey. The man who had received the five talents went at once and put his money to work and gained five more. So also, the one with the two talents gained two more. But the man who had received the one talent went off, dug a hole in the ground and hid his master's money.

"After a long time the master of those servants returned and settled accounts with them. The man who had received the five talents brought the other five. 'Master,' he said, 'you entrusted me with five talents. See, I have gained five more.'

"His master replied, 'Well done, good and faithful servant! You have been faithful with a few things; I will put you in charge of many things. Come and share your master's happiness!'

"The man with the two talents also came. 'Master,' he said, 'you entrusted me with two talents; see, I have gained two more.'

"His master replied, 'Well done, good and faithful servant! You have been faithful with a few things; I will put you in charge of many things. Come and share your master's happiness!'

"Then the man who had received the one talent came. 'Master,' he said, 'I knew that you are a hard man, harvesting where you have not sown and gathering where you have not scattered seed.

So I was afraid and went out and hid your talent in the ground. See, here is what belongs to you.'

"His master replied, 'You wicked, lazy servant! So you knew that I harvest where I have not sown and gather where I have not scattered seed? Well then, you should have put my money on deposit with the bankers, so that when I returned I would have received it back with interest.

"'Take the talent from him and give it to the one who has the ten talents.

For everyone who has will be given more, and he will have an abundance.'"

Matthew 25:14–29

Nothing before, nothing behind;
  The steps of faith
Fall on the seeming void, and find
  The rock beneath.

John Greenleaf Whittier

Jesus said, "I tell you the truth, if you have faith as small as a mustard seed, you can say to this mountain, 'Move from here to there' and it will move. Nothing will be impossible for you."

Matthew 17:20

Faith is not knowing what the future holds, but knowing who holds the future.

Author Unknown

Everything is possible for him who believes.

MARK 9:23

Because of the LORD's great love we are not consumed,
    for his compassions never fail.
They are new every morning;
    great is your faithfulness.

You, O LORD, are a compassionate
        and gracious God,
slow to anger, abounding in love
    and faithfulness.

Psalm 86:15

Strong Son of God, immortal Love,
Whom we, that have not seen thy face,
By faith, and faith alone, embrace,
Believing where we cannot prove.

Alfred, Lord Tennyson

Let us hold unswervingly to the hope we profess, for God who promised is faithful.

Hebrews 10:23

Let us step into the darkness and reach out for the hand of God. The path of faith and darkness is so much safer than the one we would choose by sight.

George Macdonald

A simple, childlike faith in the Divine Friend solves all the problems that come to us by land or sea.

Helen Keller

gentleness

*L*et your gentleness

be evident to all.

The Lord is near.

PHILIPPIANS 4:5

TERRIBLE AND GENTLE

The combination of great power and great restraint—indeed, the combination of opposite qualities and uses generally—is well-known in civilized life and in the laws of nature. The fire that warms the room when properly regulated, will, if abused, reduce the proudest palaces to ashes. The river, which softens and refreshes the landscape, if allowed to escape its banks, can devastate the most fruitful fields.

The prophet Isaiah confronts us with the highest expression of the same truth: The mighty God is the everlasting Father; the terrible One is more gentle than the gentlest friend; he who rides in the chariot of thunder stoops to lead the blind by a way that they know not and to gather the lambs in his bosom.

In pointing out the terribleness of God, I do not appeal to fear. We do not say, "Be good, or God will crush you." That is not virtue, that is not liberty—it is vice put on its good behavior. It is iniquity with a sword suspended over its head.

The great truth to be learned is that all the terribleness of God is the good person's security. When the good person sees God wasting the mountains and the hills, and drying up the rivers, he does not say, "I must worship him or he will destroy me." He says, "The beneficent side of that power is all mine. Because of that power I am safe. The very lightning is my guardian, and in the whirlwind I hear a pledge of benediction."

Joseph Parker

In thy right hand carry gentle
peace to silence envious tongues.
Be just, and fear not.

William Shakespeare

It is only imperfection that
complains of what is imperfect.
The more perfect we are, the more
gentle and quiet we become
toward the defects of others.

François Fénelon

Nothing is so strong as
gentleness, nothing so
gentle as real strength.

Francis de Sales

The gentle
mind by
gentle deeds
is known.

EDMUND SPENSER

The word of the LORD came to him: "What are you doing here, Elijah?"

He replied, "I have been very zealous for the LORD God Almighty. The Israelites have rejected your covenant, broken down your altars, and put your prophets to death with the sword. I am the only one left, and now they are trying to kill me too."

The LORD said, "Go out and stand on the mountain in the presence of the LORD, for the LORD is about to pass by."

Then a great and powerful wind tore the mountains apart and shattered the rocks before the LORD, but the LORD was not in the wind. After the wind there was an earthquake, but the LORD was not in the earthquake. After the earthquake came a fire, but the LORD was not in the fire. And after the fire came a gentle whisper.

When Elijah heard it, he pulled his cloak over his face and went out and stood at the mouth of the cave.

Then a voice said to him, "What are you doing here, Elijah?"

1 Kings 19:9–13

Speak gently! 'tis a little thing
    Dropp'd in the heart's deep well;
The good, the joy, that it may bring
    Eternity shall tell.

G. W. Langford

*In your hearts set apart Christ as Lord.
Always be prepared to give an answer to
everyone who asks you to give the reason
for the hope that you have. But do this
with gentleness and respect.*

1 Peter 3:15

GOD'S MIGHTY GENTLENESS

They say there is a hollow, safe and still,
    A point of coolness and repose
Within the center of a flame, where life might dwell
Unharmed and unconsumed, as in a luminous shell,
    Which the bright walls of fire enclose
In breachless splendor, barrier that no foes
    Could pass at will.
There is a point of rest
At the great center of the cyclone's force,
    A silence at its secret source; —
A little child might slumber undistressed,
Without the ruffle of one fairy curl,
In that strange central calm amid the mighty whirl.

So in the center of these thoughts of God,
Cyclones of power, consuming glory-fire, —
    As we fall o'erawed
Upon our faces, and are lifted higher

By His great gentleness, and carried nigher
Than unredeemèd angels, till we stand
    Even in the hollow of His hand, —
    Nay more! we lean upon His breast
There, there we find a point of perfect rest
    And glorious safety. There we see
    His thoughts to us-ward, thoughts of peace
That stoop to tenderest love; that still increase
With increase of our need; that never change,
That never fail, or falter, or forget.
             O pity infinite!
             O royal mercy free!
    O gentle climax of the depth and height
Of God's most precious thoughts, most wonderful,
       most strange!
    'For I am poor and needy,' yet
The Lord Himself, Jehovah, thinketh upon me!

Frances Ridley Havergal

As God's chosen people, holy and dearly loved, clothe yourselves with compassion, kindness, humility, gentleness and patience.

Colossians 3:12

As Thy coming was in peace,
Quiet, full of gentleness,
Let the same mind dwell in me
That was ever found in Thee.

Heinrich Held

Jesus said, "Take my yoke upon you and learn from me, for I am gentle and humble in heart, and you will find rest for your souls. For my yoke is easy and my burden is light."

Matthew 11:29–30

*A gentle
answer turns
away wrath.*

When you encounter difficulties and contradictions, do not try to break them, but bend them with gentleness and time.

Francis de Sales

Pursue righteousness, godliness, faith, love, endurance and gentleness. Fight the good fight of the faith.

1 Timothy 6:11–12

Your inner self, the unfading beauty of a gentle and quiet spirit, ... is of great worth in God's sight.

1 Peter 3:4

Gentleness and love and trust
Prevail o'er angry wave and gust.

Henry Wadsworth Longfellow

To awaken each morning with a smile brightening my face; to greet the day with reverence for the opportunities it contains; to approach my work with a clean mind; to hold ever before me, even in the doing of little things, the Ultimate Purpose toward which I am working; to meet men and women with laughter on my lips and love in my heart; to be gentle, kind, and courteous through all the hours; to approach the night with weariness that ever woos sleep and the joy that comes from work well done—this is how I desire to waste wisely my days.

Thomas Dekker

self-control

*M*ake every effort to add...

to your knowledge,

self-control; and to self-control

perseverance; and to

perseverance, godliness;

and to godliness, brotherly

kindness; and to brotherly

kindness, love.

2 PETER 1:5–7

A True Hero

Here's a hand to the woman who has courage
    To do what she knows to be right;
When she falls in the way of temptation,
    She has a hard battle to fight.
Who strives against self and her peers
    Will find a most powerful foe.
All honor to her if she conquers.
    A cheer for the woman who says "No!"

There's many a battle fought daily
    The world knows nothing about;
There's many a brave, steadfast soldier
    Whose strength puts a legion to rout.
And she who fights sin singlehanded
    Is more of a heroine, I say,
That he who leads soldiers to battle
    And conquers by arms in the fray.

Be steadfast, dear one, when you're tempted,
  To do what you know to be right.
Stand firm in love of your Savior
  And you will o'ercome in the fight.

"The right," be your battle cry ever
  In waging the warfare of life,
And God, who knows who are the heroes,
  Will give you the strength for the strife.

Based on a poem by Phoebe Cary

I count him braver who over-
comes his desires than him
who conquers his enemies; for
the hardest victory is the
victory over self.

Aristotle

Buy the truth and do not sell it;
  get wisdom, discipline and understanding.

Proverbs 23:23

While we may not be able to control
all that happens to us, we can control
what happens inside us.

Benjamin Franklin

Anyone who has knowledge controls his words.

PROVERBS 17:27 NIrV

Our fathers disciplined us for a little while as they thought best; but God disciplines us for our good, that we may share in his holiness. No discipline seems pleasant at the time, but painful. Later on, however, it produces a harvest of righteousness and peace for those who have been trained by it.

Hebrews 12:10–11

Liberty exists in proportion to wholesome restraint.

Daniel Webster

He got the better of himself, and that's the best kind of victory one can wish for.

Miguel de Cervantes

He who heeds discipline shows the way to life.

Proverbs 10:17

Maturity is:

the ability to stick with a job until it's finished;

the ability to do a job without being supervised;

the ability to carry money without spending it; and

the ability to bear an injustice without wanting to get even.

Abigail Van Buren

Thank God every morning when you get up that you have something to do which must be done, whether you like it or not. Being forced to work, and forced to do your best, will breed in you temperance, self-control, diligence, strength of will, contentment, and a hundred other virtues which the idle never know.

Charles Kingsley

He that would be superior to external influences must first become superior to his own passions.

Samuel Johnson

Good habits result from resisting temptation.

ANCIENT PROVERB

Jesus said, "I am the true vine, and my Father is the gardener. He cuts off every branch in me that bears no fruit, while every branch that does bear fruit he prunes so that it will be even more fruitful....

Remain in me, and I will remain in you. No branch can bear fruit by itself; it must remain in the vine. Neither can you bear fruit unless you remain in me. I am the vine; you are the branches. If a man remains in me and I in him, he will bear much fruit; apart from me you can do nothing.... If you remain in me and my words remain in you, ask whatever you wish, and it will be given you. This is to my Father's glory, that you bear much fruit, showing yourselves to be my disciples."

John 15:1–2, 4–5, 7–8